LLL (Love, Life, and Loss)

Ifsita Suha

Presentation by *BookLeaf Publishing*

Web: www.bookleafpub.com

E-mail: info@bookleafpub.com

ISBN: 9789357740197

First edition 2023

For my mother, my moon.

Loyal

I talked to the moon tonight.
She's very loyal, isn't she?
She was surrounded by gray clouds,
trying to tear her down.
The black sky suffocated her,
broke her off into crescents.
But she never did leave.
She listened to me with every broken piece.
She still gave me her light,
even as darkness consumed her.
She's very loyal, isn't she?

Luciform

Even if you are a threatening wave of thunder,
and I am a fleeing bird,
I will not fly away from you.
I will not run or hide.
Instead, I will fly towards you.
I will run to you and let you find me.
I will embrace you with my wings,
and calm your thundering rage.
Because you are the one who has stayed hidden
for long.
You fear striking others with your lightning.
You fear being abandoned because of your
warning thunder.
You fear being feared.
But you are not to be feared.
The heavy, dark clouds around you aren't a sign
of danger.
Rather, they are a home,
They shield your vulnerability.
The lighting that you emit is not a weapon.
Rather, it is your lone hand reaching out for any
form of love.
Your thunder is not a warning.
Rather, it is a song.
Your shadows are my light.

You are my every light.
The sun, the moon, the stars.
Your beauty is not to be feared.

Solitary

I sometimes wonder
if the moon gets tired.
Yes, the moon never fails to light up the night
sky.
The moon has been floating in the galaxy for so
long now.
The moon has seen everything in history—
but hasn't the moon seen too much?
Her wings must ache from holding it up.
She must be blinded by the sun.
She rarely feels whole.
Her full form gets cut off into crescents.
She is forced to be hidden behind the clouds.
She never feels completely whole, does she?
She must be exhausted…
I sometimes wonder
If the moon can hear me tell her
How I understand her.

Ill-fated

The sun and the moon are lovers.
Ill-fated lovers, to say the least.
The sun rises up like a bird in the sky.
The moon is a broken ship at sea and sinks
down.
They send their kisses goodbye through their
colorful cries—
Tears of pinks, oranges, purples, and deep blues.
Sunrise and sunset.
Dusk and dawn.
But fate happens to have the slightest bit of
mercy left.
In a rare eclipse,
it allows the sun and moon to meet,
each on opposite sides,
with their opposite lives,
The sun lights the moon.
And the moon accepts the sun's embrace
with loving arms.
And the world turns gold
at their meeting.

Falling

How I envy the clouds greatly.
Whatever they carry falls.
I wish I was one.
So when everything feels too heavy to bear,
I could fall to you
in rivets of rain.
I could seep into your beauty,
and you would finally be able to feel my
embrace.
Or, I could fall to you
in a soft drizzle of snow.
I could be carried in your hands
and you would finally be able to feel
how I melt in your warmth.
How I wish I was a cloud.
So all of me could fall to you.

Acatalepsy

There are many wonders of the universe.
Wonders which great minds cannot comprehend.
What is space?
How did the greatest stars come to be?
Is there a mighty force which has created the
universe?
Or is the universe itself, a creator?
I am not one of the great minds.
I do not question the universe, itself.
What I do seek answers to, however,
is the endless amount of beauty in you.
It is the most everlasting in my eyes.
It cannot compare to the infinity of the universe.
My mind and soul tries day and night
to fathom the beauty of your symmetry–
The symmetry which the equations of the
universe cannot compare with.
I want to take you to the other galaxies,
where the dust of the stars full our lungs,
where shooting asteroids are the only thing in
our way,
where I can mock the deepest black holes,
because they will never spiral as deep as your
eyes do.
The puzzling beauty of the universe
cannot compare to the complexity of your soul.

Logophile

They ask me,
"What are you if not a writer?"
"I am mute," I want to reply.
"I am love-less," I want to reply.
Because it is not my voice which speaks.
Rather, it is my hand, a railway to my mind.
The ink which spills from my pen are the
pathways to my worlds.
My worlds contain my words.
And my words are the language of my soul.
Everything I love does not know I do
because my soul is silent,
and so are the words which reside in them.
So if not a writer,
I am simply an empty, wandering being.
I am love-less and I am mute.

Granted

When I said you are my everything,
I always meant it.
But I never truly knew what it meant.
Were you the blood which rushed through my
veins?
Were you a piece of my heart?
Were you the fresh air around me?
I never truly knew then,
but now I do.
Because you have crumbled into stardust,
and now your constellations stare down at me
who sits alone.
I have been thinking about the truth since then.
Now I have realized.
You were the boulders which blocked the rivers
from crashing down upon me,
but now the rivers run loose and drench me head
to toe, and even to the pits of my soul.
You were my sun which rose after a long, dark
night,
but here I lay now under a never-ending black
sky.
You were the rain to my flowers, turning me, a
mere seed, into a bright red rose,

but now I weep my own rain and my brown,
shriveled petals fall one by one.
You were the roots of my tree, because with
your strength, I was able to withstand all
disaster,
but now I scatter in ruins, broken down by a
storm.
I realized a little too late
what you truly were.

Forever

If there is a next life,
I want to be reborn as the Earth,
and I would make you the moon,
so I may gaze up at you every night.
Maybe then, our forever could actually last
forever.
Even if the sun takes over the day sky,
I would be okay with that,
because I would know that you are still there,
perhaps hiding,
perhaps tugging at my heart to see how much I'd
miss you.
Then, I would let the wind carry up my whispers
to you,
"I will miss you forever."
And when the night sky returns at last,
I would take you into my arms,
and you would let your illumination carry your
whispers down to me,
"I will be here forever."

Ticking

Tick, Tick, Tick.
I still hear the clock ticking in my head.
It's repetitive and maddening,
yet somehow it brings me peace.
The clock lays broken on my window seat.
The deep blue light reflects upon the shattered
glass.
I sometimes see your reflection in them.
I can see your smile in the cracks.
I see your eyes within the moonlight which casts
upon the surface.
But there is something missing:
Your voice.
I cannot hear the ticks of your voice.
I look down at the clock, tears seeping through
the cracks.
I cry as much as I can
so that my tears can bash the hands of the clock.
But my tears are as weak as I am.
They cannot make the clock tick.
They cannot return your voice.
It is all inside my head,
because the only thing truly in my embrace,
is the lifeless clock taunting me in silence,
and yet, it is still alive in my head.

Ticking,
Ticking,
Ticking.

People

I have always been fond of people.
But I don't mean as in I am fond of exchanging
different conversations with many people.
I mean, I am fond of pondering upon the life
within people.
I watch and wonder rather than join and engage.
I am fond of diving into one's eyes and exploring
what's hidden beneath
as opposed to taking a quick glance and
skimming over the surface.
I look at many things and I wonder about many
things.
I look at a student reading a book on the bus,
and I wonder if there is magic tingling at the tips
of their fingers,
or what fantastical creatures are roaming in their
head.
I look at a laughing couple walking at a park,
and I wonder how many tears have slipped in the
in-between moments,
or whether one has a ring tucked up their sleeve.
I look at an elderly woman sitting alone on a
bench,
and I wonder when the last time she received a
phone call was,

or if she is simply breathing in her old memories
from the air around her.
I look at a rather quiet person sitting in the midst
of a crowded, chattering room,
and I wonder if they are carrying boulders of
burdens on their back,
or if they are dancing in a distant daydream.
I look around me, and see so many different
kinds of people.
Some laugh, some quietly smile, some frown,
and some are unreadable.
But I wonder if the stars from different galaxies
can see the stars shining deep within every
individual.
I wonder if everyone knows
that each life is making the world shine
with billions of lights.

Blooming

Us humans in pain are a lot like blooming
flowers.
When our pain is too unbearably heavy to carry,
our souls bleed from our tearful eyes.
Just as when clouds pour when they hold too
much.
Our tears fall into our cupped hands and seep
into our skin,
and the rain drops on flowers repeatedly before
sinking into the soil beneath.
Our tears do hurt, they pound on us,
and so do the petals of a flower as they get
beaten up by droplets of rain.
But in the end,
our tears dry themselves, only leaving invisible
scars which remind us of our strength–
Our strength to be able to release everything
pent up.
The rain trails deep into the soil as the ground
surface dries.
The flowers bloom,
and so do we.
Because the most beautiful of flowers
were raised by the rain
that came before the sun.

Blue

Everyone here is yellow,
bright sunshine and singing birds.
They are light emerging from the clouds.
But why am I still a heavy cloud stuck here,
all blue and gray?
Why must you have taken the sun with you
when you left?
Why must you have taken your voice from my
memory
so that I will never hear your song once more?
Why must you have taken my soul,
intertwined with yours?
I am deep blue and gray surrounded by yellow,
a crippled flower untouched by all birds,
a cloud,
Far, Far away
from the sun.

Wind

I don't envy anything else
as much as I envy the wind.
Because it wraps around you
eternally
Just as I wish I could.
It makes you feel more than I ever can.
I envy the wind's fingers, as they can reach to
you
and tuck away your hair, fallen over your eyes.
The wind gets to admire those eyes with no fear.
I envy the wind's lips, as they can shower
endless kisses
on you, making you smile at the ticklish feel.
How I wish I could hear your laugh
as much as the wind does
My, how the wind is so invisibly lucky.

Winter

Be my winter, my love.
Take your hands and put them into my pockets.
Take mine into the sleeves of your coat.
Let your red nose tickle mine
so that the flakes of snow on us melt away.
Whisper to me, "I love you,"
and let the cold winds freeze your words
so that I can see the clouds of your love.
Lean so close to me, that the air of winter
becomes fearful
of the warmth in-between us
Become my winter warmth, my love.

Haunt

I have never understood
why the lost must drift apart from this world.
Does the other universe hold such serenity,
that it erases your memory of this world?
Do you see a utopia so beautiful,
that you no longer wish to see me?
You said then, that you will always be with me.
Then haunt me!
Let your stolen words escape to me.
Let your tears fall down from a tree.
Shout so loud that I will flee.
Just do not leave me in this never ending spiral
of questions,
where I cannot hear you,
feel you,
or see you
for eternity.

Immortal

Because my love is forever yours,
You will live forever.
Even if the Heavens fall for you
and wish to take your hand.
Because you will always reside within my
pages.
Your smile will live in the torn holes of my
papers.
Your voice will take the form of the waves of
my ink.
Your memory will fill all of my journals.
So, my love,
do not fear death,
as I have made you immortal with my words.

Missing

"You are missing from me,"
I think that is a better way to say "I miss you."
Because you were not just my heart's
companion, no.
You were a piece of my heart.
But now, there is a void, empty hole where you
used to reside.
It lays abandoned and broken down.
Cobwebs wrap around my heart.
Vines and roots crack through the walls.
Thorns prick at anything else which tries to
enter.
A piece of you is missing from me,
and it cannot be replaced.
So, abandoned is what my heart will remain.

Youniverse

I look at you, my love,
and I see the universe.
Life must have truly fallen for you,
because it gave away the most magical pieces of
itself to you.
Life stole the universe's brightest stars,
and put them into your eyes.
Life stole the universe's greatest galaxies,
and weaved them into your soul.
Life stole the deepest black holes.
and made space in your heart for them.
Life has made you with all the magic there is.

Longing

What other love is more passionate
than that of the trees and the clouds?
How madly the clouds fell,
and how loyal the trees are.
Summertime sends blessings upon the trees.
Warmth seeps into the branches and soil
beneath.
Color dances upon the leaves vibrantly.
The aura of green lifts into the sky,
high enough for the clouds to embrace.
The clouds take in the life of the trees from
above.
But then autumn arrives and drains the life from
the leaves of the trees.
The leaves shrivel and they whither from their
branches.
And the clouds can do nothing but watch in
agony
As their trees slowly lose the suns in their eyes.
And then winter arrives, the most deadly.
It takes whatever remains of the life within the
trees.
It strikes their branches bare
and its cruel, cold hands hold the trees back,
frozen

so that they cannot reach out to their clouds.
All the trees can do is gather their love within their roots,
far hidden so that nothing can steal it away.
The trees send a silent prayer to the clouds,
praying that the clouds wait for them to come back to life.
But that is when the clouds grow impatient.
The pain of not being able to feel their trees grows too heavy,
and the clouds bleed their tears.
The clouds rain, and rain, and rain.
Yet somehow their pain cannot pass.
So the clouds grow angry.
They curse at their enemies, the cold, through their thunder.
They wish to strike destiny with their lighting.
The clouds storm, and storm, and storm.
And the trees can do nothing but watch tearfully
as their beloved clouds become restless
for the spring to arrive.
But despite their agony, rage, and longing,
deep down, they know that their hope will arrive.
Spring.
Spring arrives after a never-ending winter.
It gives life back to the trees.
And the trees and the clouds rejoice once they are reunited again.

Lasting

Nothing ever lasts forever.
It is a tragic thing to think about—
At surface level, at least.
It is undeniable that someday, everything we know
will wither away.
The stars that we send our wishes to
will someday fall into dust.
The sun which we seek guidance from
will someday grow tired, and wear out.
The moon which we share our sorrow with
will someday take our pain in its arms along
with its own
and drift off into the darkness of infinity.
Even these pages, where your eyes lay
will someday crumble deep into the Earth.
Eventually, everything will wither,
and you will wonder with tearful eyes,
if anything was even worth the loss.
Yes, my dear.
Everything will be worth the loss.
Because:
Even if the stars fall,
they will know that your wishes were listened to.
Even if the sun wears out,

it will go to sleep peacefully, knowing that its
light has guided you when it rose.
Even if the moon drifts away,
it will carry your tears in its arms, knowing that
it was by you when no one else was.
Even if these pages crumble,
their words, even if just two, will reside in
someone's heart.
Everything does end.
But, we can smile despite the tears
because everything at least happened.

www.ingramcontent.com/pod-product-compliance
Lightning Source LLC
La Vergne TN
LVHW021349200726
843509LV00014B/2761